With a Mind to Achieve

By

Wayne Jarman

WITH A MIND TO ACHIEVE

Written by Wayne Jarman

Published by AWL Media

74 Fletcher Street
Edgeworth NSW 2285
Australia

Website: www.ReflectiveBubble.com

First printed March 2011
Copyright Wayne Jarman

ISBN 978-0-9870931-0-3

TO LINDI, my best friend and soul mate. Thank you for your support and love.

CONTENTS

PREFACE

The reality of life is that there is more than one reality. In fact, there are as many realities on this Earth as there are beings on this Earth.

We all view reality (whatever that is) through our physical senses, through our experiences, through our mental processes.

What I perceive as reality is very different to what you perceive as reality.

Already, you might have gleaned that this is going to be a very different read. You may not like this book. You may not like me. You may not get to the last page. (I hope you will.) You may often wonder 'what is this guy on?' Remember …this is my reality – and it works for me!

If you read this book as I have intended it to be read, it may take years. There are books within this book …References to books and wonderful minds that have affected my mind. I recommend them to you.

The greatest battle of your life is the battle to control your mind – to own your thoughts and to keep them positive and supportive of you. Lose that battle and live a life of anguish …a life of wondering 'why me?'

Win that battle and the rewards could be beyond your imagination …a life of success, living great experiences and achieving great things. I wish that for you.

Welcome to my book.

THE JOURNEY SO FAR

It's not about me!

This book is about life and finding your individual path. My path and your path are not the same and they are different to the path of everyone else on this planet. I don't mean to indicate, by briefly telling my story, that I am anything special or that my actions or thoughts should be duplicated.

This short history of me is only intended as an introduction. If you decide that you don't relate to this person or you decide that his life isn't anything special, then that's fine. Keep reading anyway. The book is not about me. It's about provoking thoughts about life.

No two lives are the same. No two people are sitting on the same point of their personal development. I don't see personal development as one linear line, anyway. It is a series of parallel lines with each line representing a facet of life …Achievements, Health, Wealth, Relationships, etc.

One person can be well along the line in Achievements but well back on the Relationships and Health lines. Another person may have great relationships but be broke financially. How do you compare these two people? The short answer is that you don't. If I have learnt anything so far, it is that you don't compare yourself to others. You only compare yourself to you.

Don't compare yourself to others.

By comparing yourself to others you always compare your inside (fears, doubts, insecurities, lack of confidence) with their outside (mask). It will never be a fair comparison. Even if you find someone who you shine next to, what is the point of the comparison? Help them shine like you and then, and only then, there may have been a point.

This bit is about me:

Briefly ...I was blessed. I was born into a loving family to wonderful parents in a beautiful, free country and I was encouraged to learn, respect and love.

I had two childhoods in one.

The son of a wharf laborer, I was brought up in one of the docks suburbs of Newcastle NSW Australia. There, on week days, I learnt how to play hard, fight and judge my peers and teachers.

On the weekends, my parents and I vanished to a small area of Port Stephens called North Arm Cove. In the 1950s to late 1970s this area was an isolated, unserviced (no phone, no electricity, no piped water), pristine cove with only a handful of weekenders situated between bush and water. There, on weekends, I learnt how to be alone, to walk and think in silence, to fish, to appreciate the beauty of nature and to feel part of the universe.

If there was any point to regrets in this world then I might regret that, in this hectic time in history, I could not give my children the same peaceful childhood existence that I had in that small cove.

There is no point to regrets.

(I remain in awe of nature. I cannot begin to believe that this marvelous world has occurred by accident. I hasten to add, however, that I do not belong to any religion and that I fail so badly as a philosopher that thinking how the world was created and who created the creator, only makes my brain hurt.)

Much, much later in life, I unlearned the awful skill of judging my peers and teachers. I now leave all judgment to a higher being than I and accept my fellow beings as equals – no greater or lesser than I and with faults, like mine, that make us all human. When I eliminated judgment from my life and prepared myself to be a student, the teachers came into my life.

Eliminate judgment, become a student, look for the teachers to arrive.

So where am I on my personal development path? Oh …I'm in there somewhere. Am I a great teacher of fellow life travelers? No, I don't think so. Am I preparing to be someone's guru? Not likely! Nor am I preparing to ascend or take on sainthood. In fact, I haven't found anyone in that category. I have found, however, some wonderful teachers who I have learned a great deal from. Perhaps I can thank them by passing on some of what I have learned.

I have worked in heavy industry (steel, hydraulics, mining) for most of my working life. I have been a Laborer, a Storeman, a Purchasing Officer, an Engineer. I have been promoted, retrenched, unemployed and self-employed.

I have been stressed, angry and hostile and I have held my wife and children in my arms and loved them and felt their love.

I've trod the boards as an amateur actor. I've stroked my ego in a political party, I've written the unpublished works seeking fame and fortune.

In short, I am just an ordinary person who has experienced enough of life to look back and make some notes. I hope that you may find them useful in your life, whether you find something that you can take on board or something that you can avoid.

So what was the point of my fifty (and some more) years on this planet?

Nothing really!

I'm not depressed as I write this. I am simply being honest.

When you consider the vastness of the universe and each individual's limited lifespan and even the limited lifespan of this planet and the human race, then the stuff that we go through on a daily basis doesn't really matter. All the stress, all the heartache, all the tears and struggle, the bad times, the good times …for what?

(You could be forgiven for thinking at this stage …Well, what's the point of reading this book? Good question! But now that you've read this far …just keep reading.)

However, next time you are about to blow a piffle valve over some irritation, just remember this point.

The 'stuff' doesn't really matter.

In the great scheme of events, your irritations really don't matter. On the surface of things, this may not sound like great news to you. However, I found this to be the most liberating information that I have ever encountered. I no longer need to react with anger or stress when something goes wrong. It is simply an event in my life and I can always choose to sit placidly, reflect on what has happened, and think "it doesn't matter".

Having made this comment, there must be some purpose. We all need something to hold onto to make our lives meaningful.

I have found my something, …my anchor.

Read on.

WHAT IS THE PURPOSE OF THIS?

Philosophers throughout the ages (including that great sage, Monty Python) have asked the question "What is the meaning of life?

Of course, there is no definite answer. No matter how well educated a person may be, they cannot logically answer the unanswerable. The pessimist will look at this and think how terrible it is that, while we remain alive, there will never be a definite answer. Those who want to step over to my side of the line will think "That's great. That means my theory is as good as any theory that the greatest thinkers of the world can compile".

So if we cannot logically answer the unanswerable, what can we do?

Step one: Stop being logical.

There is more to this world and universe than logic. I know that there is a lot of logical discipline involved in understanding what happens within our physical universe but there are also times that the human race can only turn to 'gut feeling' and faith (as it has over the eons).

However, if we are going to turn to this undisciplined approach of gut feeling and faith, please have the respect for your fellow human being to allow him to have a different gut feeling or faith (belief) to your belief.

Too many wars have been fought and too many poor souls persecuted because their unsubstantiated belief was different to the unsubstantiated belief of someone else.

I remember standing in a Christian church. I occasionally end up in those places for Christenings, Weddings and Funerals. On this occasion, it was a Funeral. The minister was speaking of the life of the lady who had died. (She was a lovely lady - Lindi's great aunt – who I have many fond memories of) and he made the comment that "here was a lady who had known her purpose in life". I don't know why he believed that he knew this but his words certainly moved my thoughts down a different path to where they had been previously.

I remember thinking "If that were true, she would have been a very fortunate lady."

And in that very peaceful environment, at a time when I was feeling close to my God (whoever and whatever 'God' may be), my mind sulkily pushed forward the thought "I wish I knew what my purpose was".

Immediately and in a very different 'tone', a voice raced through my mind with the words "Well why don't you ask?"

It wasn't a simple, bland question. It was asked in a manner of frustration and annoyance that was responding to the sulkiness of my question. The intent was more along the lines of "Well why don't you ask? ...you dummy!"

It took me by surprise and I decided to take action when I next had the opportunity. I returned to concentrating on the funeral service.

Later that day, I put on some relaxing music, made myself comfortable on my lounge, closed my eyes and allowed my mind to become calm.

(Some people may call this meditation. I avoid the term because there are so many definitions of meditation and so many different styles of meditation, and so many people with hang-ups about meditation that you can usually end up with strange looks and convoluted conversations just by dropping the word into a sentence. It's like the snobbery ritual that some people place on the drinking of red wine. You can find lots of people very willing to look down their nose at you because you just have a simple desire to enjoy drinking the wine, but, back to the story ...)

When I was relaxed, I simply asked the question "What is my purpose in life?" and I received an answer that provided me with two missions to achieve. I am not prepared to share those missions here but this book is part of the process.

The point is: It was that simple!

Ask and you will receive.

I don't want to get biblical on you, but Jesus (and Buddha before him) came to town with some very simple, basic messages that the human race has gone to extraordinary lengths to complicate ever since.

Feel free to ask what you want to know!

Feel free to ask for what you want!

Now, if you don't normally take time to sit quietly and you're normally stressed, your mind may not be ready to have this sort of communication. It may take some practice, perhaps over a period of months, in sitting quietly and de-stressing before you feel comfortable to ask questions.

You, the reader, may be cynically asking now "Who am I supposed to be talking to?"

My immediate answer is "I don't care". There are so many beliefs associated with a human's spirituality that a book could be written (not by me) on the huge variety and it's another occasion of "It doesn't matter!"

Depending on your particular beliefs (that themselves are dependent on the path that your life has followed to this point), you could be talking with:

- your own subconscious mind,
- your higher self,
- your spirit guides,
- your angels,
- your departed loved ones,
- Buddha,
- Jesus,
- God,
- Others that I have not listed (with sincere apologies).

It doesn't matter who you are talking to. Just ask the questions and see what replies may come.

So, returning to the question of "What is the purpose of this?", my comment in the last chapter of "Nothing really matters" was meant to refer to "the stuff". By this I mean the things that happen to you and around you …your circumstances.

One day, your time on this earth will be through (and a large proportion of our fellow space travelers go through life blocking this fact from their thoughts). Afterwards there will be 'things' to be distributed among family and friends and a lump of decaying flesh that the appropriate people will have to dispose of in the socially acceptable way. You won't be concerned with any of this.

You will be left with nothing but you ...whoever 'you' is.

Here is where the theories all get very messy and contradictory. Various religions have various beliefs. If you're like me and don't subscribe to any particular religious belief, then you will have developed your own Spiritual beliefs or even a belief that says that you do not exist at all at this point.

I hold the belief that I, whoever 'I' is, will remain in spirit form. Spirit? Soul? Identity? Whatever! Where that form will reside I do not know.

Something that is very important to me is:

If I am stuck with me for the rest of eternity, I want to like me.

Can you imagine going through eternity with someone you don't like, even if it is yourself.

Therefore, what does matter while I am on this earth is that I do things, say things, think things that I am not ashamed of. Even better ...that I am proud of. I want to be able to look at me in the mirror and think "I like this person. I respect this person." I want to grow so that, eventually, I will be better than I am now.

Therefore, while the 'stuff' that happens to me doesn't matter, it matters to me that I grow better. To answer the question 'What is the purpose of this?':

One of my purposes is "to grow".

If I grow and I have principles and morals that I respect in me, then I can bear my company for the rest of eternity. Problem solved.

My next problem is that all of the other spirits, souls, entities that I previously shared this world with might end up in the same place as me. (I don't believe in a distinct heaven and hell. They are religious creations to control the masses. My God loves all of us, unconditionally.)

To put it bluntly:

If I am stuck with you for the rest of eternity, I want to like you.

It provides a new perspective on helping others to 'grow', doesn't it?

I once belonged to a Toastmasters group. I loved to watch people grow in confidence and abilities. It felt good to be part of the support group that made a difference in other peoples' lives. Because of those good feelings, I later spent time at my children's high school running Youth Leadership courses. Lindi and I later joined with friends and had some wonderful times running Personal Development courses.

Those of us in this world who like to assist other people to develop and grow get a kick out of the process and the result. It has never been a totally unselfish act. Even less so now, when you consider the urgent need for everyone around you to grow.

Another of my purposes is "to help others to grow".

I use the word 'help' intentionally. We cannot 'make' or 'drag' or 'push'. The person must be willing to grow – and, then, we can lead by example.

'To lead' isn't 'to talk about' the right principles, the right behaviour. 'To lead' is 'to display'. It amazes me that I live in a society where our elected leaders tell us lies …and we know they tell us lies …and they know that we know that they tell us lies …yadda yadda yadda. And yet, people wonder at the principles of people in our society and the *supposed* lack of respect and lack of direction of the young people. To have principles in a society, a society needs principled leadership. To lead someone, you must continually display your commitment to living what you are suggesting to them.

Walk the Talk.

As to the question of why am I here at all …

I was asleep in bed. In my dream I was asking questions of a 'higher being'. Questions that I had forgotten by the time I awoke. But I remembered the last question because the being asked it of me.

"Why?", the being asked. (Implying the age old question of "Why am I? Why do I exist?")

I replied, "Because if I wasn't, I couldn't. To do I must be."

I had disturbed Lindi and I explained the dialogue that had taken place. She was sufficiently impressed (for that hour of the morning) but wanted to know more. "Ask why we <u>want</u> to do."

Before I was fully asleep, the answer came. Words fail to fit the thoughts and emotions that came through in my slumber, but below is the best fit that I can provide:

"Because in the spiritual realm I cannot touch a tree or drive a car or walk on grass or concrete. The spiritual realm is where souls blend in bliss and absolute love. It is a wonderful place …but there I cannot do. There I cannot have an effect."

From this I have gleaned another purpose:

My purpose is to experience and do.

Yet so many people hide in the corner of life and wrap themselves in cotton wool – hoping that if they stay away from the experiences that life might not hurt them. Some people develop addictions (tobacco, drugs, alcohol) to help them blur the real world.

It's like paying to get into the fun park and hiding behind the toilets until its time to go home.

Get over it!

Go out and experience life. That's what we are here for!

Yes life is dangerous. It was once pointed out to me that life is so dangerous that not one of us will get out of it alive.

I'm not suggesting that you run around doing dangerous things just to risk death (I'm not a skydiver or a bungee jumper and I don't intend to be - simply because that is not my interest) but don't let fears prevent you from doing the things that you want to experience in life.

Fear is a good thing. It was designed to keep us safe. It was designed to keep us from doing things that our mind knows will harm us. When our ancestors were confronted with a charging woolly mammoth or a snarling saber-toothed tiger, it was good that they felt fear. It added adrenalin to their system that helped them run faster. But, unfortunately, the body's fear system also acts by warning us of its concerns about new events that haven't been experienced before.

18

(It sends adrenalin into our system and makes our knees shake when we just stand in front of a group of people to talk.) Make an intelligent judgment on the actual safety level and overcome the fear when you decide that these fear levels are unjustified.

One of my all time favourite books is *Feel The Fear And Do It Anyway* by Susan Jeffers. It changed my life. If you haven't read it, I highly recommend that you do so.

Recommended Reading:
Feel The Fear And Do It Anyway (Susan Jeffers).

So there it is. I am now in the same league as Monty Python. I have tried to define the meaning of life. You may think "dribble". Great! To think that, you have at least thought about the question. You may be right. I may be wrong. But if I am wrong, my theory at least gives me a firm basis for living a wonderful, fulfilling life. I will:

- Look at the stuff of circumstance and think "It doesn't matter".
- Ask for what I want and what I want to know.
- Live my life so that I like and respect myself.
- Make my purpose to grow.
- Assist others to grow.
- Experience life to the full.

BALANCE

When I was sixteen, I joined the Civil Defence (later renamed to the State Emergency Service) and remained a member for ten years. The aim of this voluntary organization is to provide trained people to assist the community during emergencies (Floods, Bush Fires, Storms, Earthquakes, Nuclear Attack – it was the 1970s after all). This is a wonderful community-orientated organisation and I enjoyed being around the great friends I made during that time. I recommend it to anyone who is looking to put something back into their community.

While I was a member, I trained in Radio and Rescue and was given the illustrious title of Deputy Intelligence Officer. This may sound very impressive but I hasten to add that there were only two members of the Intelligence Department – The intelligence Officer and his Deputy (me!) – and, to this day, I haven't been intelligent enough to work out just what this Department was meant to do. Nevertheless, a great time was had by all concerned and we did provide a service during emergencies.

One evening when I was in my late teens, I was working at the Headquarters finalising a report. The Controller of the organization (a Councilor, Past Lord Mayer and WWII Decorated Serviceman) walked past and then returned to my open door.

"Haven't you got a home to go to?"

(When an Australian asks this of you, he is simply reminding you that it's getting late and suggesting that it's time you went home to your family.)

Being only young and having had very little to do with this distinguished city identity, I very nervously explained that I was just finishing a report and would go home soon.

"That's good", he replied. Then instead of moving on he paused and looked me in the eyes. "You have to get your priorities right in this world."

I felt like I was at school and he was one of the teachers. I look back now and realize that he was being a teacher of a very different sort.

Before he moved on down the corridor, he added sadly "I didn't get mine right."

Then he was gone. I finished my report and went home.

The impact of these few words of wisdom would probably have faded and now be forgotten except that the newspapers, radio stations and TV stations, only a few days later, were reporting that he had died.

His words have stayed with me. The impact has stayed with me. How sad would it be to get to the last days of your life and decide that, despite the war medals and illustrious career (substitute your own successes in here), you got it wrong. And yet, when you think about it, probably more people would reach that decision at that point than those who decide they got it right.

(I've just returned from the bathroom after washing my eyes. I wonder if it would have made a difference to him that he made such an impact on my life that typing his words can still bring tears to my eyes over thirty years later.)

Did this event make a difference in my life? Probably. I wish I could say a resounding 'Yes'. But the answer is only 'Probably'. I still blindly followed a career path for much of my working life. I remember the conversations, on more than one occasion, with Lindi about whether we would keep trying or settle for a divorce. I look back and wonder when my little babies grew into adults. I refuse to have regrets, though. I simply accept that I did the best I could with what I knew at the time.

On the positive side, I remember making career moves based on what was best for my relationships rather than what was best for my career and pocket. As a result, I now have a wonderful, glorious relationship with Lindi and we are each other's best friend with plans of growing old together (sometime in the next hundred years) and we have a wonderful, close family.

There are many areas of your life that demand your time and energy:

- Family,
- Work / Career,
- Friends,
- Hobbies and Interests,
- Study,
- Community Involvement,
- Spiritual Growth,
- Financial Development,
- Leisure.

Balancing these and getting them in the right proportions will make a significant difference to the quality of your life. Getting the balance right will put you in the top five percent of human beings who currently reside on this planet. (Please don't go looking for the supporting statistics. This is a gut-feel figure with which you are at liberty to disagree.)

For the older readers who are now saying "Yes! But how the hell do you do that?" I empathise. For the younger readers who are wondering what the fuss is about ...read on.

I have found that it is very easy, in the bedlam and noise of this world, to become without purpose and to end up just swimming with the current. The problem with this is that the current may not be flowing in the right direction.

Step one in getting your priorities right is to work out what your priorities are. Asking yourself some basic questions might help. Questions such as:

- What is important to me?
- Who is important to me?
- What would I fight for?
- Who would I fight for?
- What would I be prepared to die for?
- Who would I be prepared to die for?

Answer these questions and you will have a clue as to what your priorities are.

(Now, if you are anything like me, you will read these questions and keep reading. NO! I recommend that you go back and answer the questions. Grab a piece of paper and write down the answers.)

This page now ends so that you can do the exercise. When you have finished, restart reading at the next page.

(If you are like me you will probably just keep reading. That's fine ...but remember I am more often, in this book, putting myself forward as the poor example that made a lot of mistakes. Follow my example if you like …or learn from my mistakes.)

If only I knew then what I know now!

Have you ever heard anyone say this? They say it because they have realised that, if they had been armed with the right information early in life, they would not have made the mistakes that they now realise they did. Wouldn't it be great if we were issued with a manual for leading a wonderful life? (Many have tried to write it. There are a lot of great books out there.)

Hindsight is a wonderful thing only if you have the opportunity to start again. When you don't have the opportunity to start over (as with life), then the next best process is to learn from other people's mistakes and to gain from their experience. As a young man I did not do this. Nobody pointed me in the direction of the right books and I didn't go looking for them. Nor did I listen to people older than me. I knew more than them. (Dumb!) Hopefully, some young person reading this book may be more intelligent than I was when I was young and just simply have more common sense than me.

Two hints:

1.   Take control of your life.

2.   Take responsibility for your life.

One of the primary sources of satisfaction in life is to be in control.

When someone else is telling you what to do and when to do it, you cannot lead a satisfying life.

The bureaucrats of this world who need to make rules to control the way that we behave are creating an environment of stress, anxiety and depression that is reflected in the depressing news that we see on our televisions of an evening. (I've stopped watching the news. I suggest for the benefit of your mental health that you do the same. If you can't solve the problem, then you shouldn't be worrying about it.) The eruptions of violence on our roads, in our schools, in a neighbour's home have a root cause in the helplessness of lack of control of a life.

The ridiculous blame setting and lawsuits that we hear of in our courts have a root cause in individual's not taking responsibility for their own actions and their own lives.

I am amazed at the number of young people that I meet who are on anti-depressant drugs. Why? Is it related to diet? Lack of a life challenge? Lack of control over their lives? All of the above?

Firmly grab hold of your life and decide what you want from it!

Another exercise (equally as important as the last):

If you were ridiculously rich and money was never a worry again, what would you do with your life? If you didn't have to work to pay the bills, (after the first week of sleeping in every day) what would you want to achieve? Who would you achieve them with? Where would you go? What would you experience? What goals would you set?

Compare this with what you do now. How far away from your real dreams is your current lifestyle?

I attended a Personal Development seminar and was asked to take part in an exercise that was an extension of an exercise that can be found in Stephen Covey's book 'The 7 Habits of Highly Effective People'.

Recommended Reading:
The 7 Habits of Highly Effective People
(Stephen R. Covey).

The exercise required me to sit quietly with my eyes closed and visualise my own funeral. (Sounds a bit morbid but it had significant benefits for me.) The plan was that I would have three speakers at my funeral:

1.   A friend,
2.   A work associate, and
3.   A family member.

At the time of doing this exercise I was managing to keep in touch with my close friends on an irregular basis while working hard in my career. I was driving for three hours a day just to get to and from work and was working long days.

Consequently, the first two speakers went well and had no surprises for me.

The third imagined speaker was my daughter who, at the time, was about twelve years old.

A little bit of background:

When my daughter, Larissa, was only about four years of age I was working six long days a week. I was also studying and was attending classes on two nights a week. This was the little girl who asked her mother "Where does Daddy sleep?" because I was leaving for work before she woke up and arriving home after she was asleep. (Isn't that ridiculous! I loved that little girl so much and wasn't even seeing her awake. Are there any readers out there...)

This was also the little girl who was sitting in the bath one afternoon when I arrived home from work unexpectedly (because I had forgotten to pack some notes that I needed to take to class) and asked me "Hello Daddy. Have you come to visit us?"

(Out of the mouths of children come some very important wake up calls! Listen out for them!)

I changed jobs not long after these wake up calls so that I could spend more time with my family. However, when I became bored with this job (about three years later), I moved back into career mode and took the job at a coal mine an hour and a half away from my home.

So Larissa at twelve years of age, the third imagined speaker at my imagined funeral, stood at the lectern and said:

"I think my Daddy was a great guy."

This was fine. But then she paused and thought before continuing.

"I *think* he was a great guy. I didn't see him very much."

I didn't like this exercise. I cried. It hurt to know that I was doing so badly in balancing my life and spending time with the people I loved. It hurt that I knew it down deep inside and I was deliberately keeping it buried and carrying on with my career regardless.

Within eighteen months I had resigned from that job and was working for myself as a Consultant in an attempt to gain some flexibility in my life that would allow more time for the people I loved. It sort of worked. Not as well as I would have hoped but things were better than they had been.

I also developed some affirmations as a result of the Personal Development course. (I am grateful to Peter and Sharon McMahon for their wonderful course.) My aim is to read these (and others) daily.

I create an excellent balance between family, work, other interests and relaxation so that my life is complete and satisfying.

I have quality time with Lindi and our beautiful family. They are the lights of my life - my encouragement for growing.

I retain regular contact with my close friends. (their friendship is very important to me.)

I occasionally <u>plan</u> to spend time on relaxation. This is necessary alpha time. Great things will result.

I am a <u>very</u> successful businessman with affluence in money and in all other areas of life. Our lifestyle is admired by those around us.

Wherever I am, I am there 100%.

These simple tools (the funeral exercise and the affirmations) made a magnificent difference in my life.

Not long after doing this course, my family and I were sitting around the table and I asked the question "Have you noticed any difference since Mum and Dad did the course?"

Gareth (about ten years old at the time) beamed. "Yea, we all love each other again."

Feedback is good. Good feedback is great!

Balance in life is the real 'balancing act'. It will not happen by accident. It is a matter of knowing what is important and continually reviewing your life to determine if you are dealing with the important things first. And then making changes, as required, to bring back the balance.

Review, Change, Find the Balance, Repeat the process.

There will always be forces that carry us away from the balance. Be ever vigilant!

I wish you even greater success than I have had.

ACHIEVEMENT

No-one is born average! We lead average lives based on the decisions that we make, or don't make, on a daily basis. Equally important, in living an average life, is to have average dreams, average goals, average ambitions – or to have no dream at all!

Get a Dream!

Everyone who has created anything in this world has created it twice – first in their mind and secondly in the physical world. Everything starts with a thought.

The old saying "You've gotta have a dream to have a dream come true" is not going out of style.

What have you thought about your life? Most of us just think about surviving on a daily basis. To achieve a better than average life, you should be asking yourself the daily question: "What do I want to do before I die?"

Young people can answer these questions with significant ease. The older people (twenty and above) may have greater difficulty – because the reality of the world has impacted on their dreaming ability.

Forget Reality! Begin with the end in mind.

For a large part of my adult life I have had trouble with this dream thing. Some people have trouble with the word itself. If you don't like 'dream', use 'goal' or 'ambition' or something similar. But whatever you do, develop one.

I have worked on the dream and I now have a list of over a hundred things that I want to achieve before I die. A small sample of my dreams is listed below. Again, it is not about me. These are examples (from an Australian male perspective) just to give you an idea of the areas that you could be developing your dreams in. Use these examples as prompts to develop your own (even if it is "Oh no, I wouldn't do that. I would prefer to ...").

I want to:
- Scuba dive on the Great Barrier Reef,
- Have a four-wheel-drive holiday around Australia,
- Sail the Whitsunday Islands,
- Have a family white Christmas in Austria,
- Visit the United Kingdom,
- Sponsor a village,
- Assist family and friends,
- Live in a large home on an acreage,
- Have a carousel on our property for our grandchildren,
- Build a rainforest,
- Retire from the job early to paint and write,
- Have books published,
- Produce films,
- Make a spiritual difference.

This is just a sampling to get your thoughts going. I don't expect them to be important to you. What do **you** want to do?

_____

_____

_____

Don't feel restricted by this page length. Grab a pad of paper!

Now that you have developed a list of 'to do before I die' items, there are some steps to be taken. In traditional goal setting, the following steps are important:

1.   Decide what you want (your list),

2.   Look at where you are now,

3.   Look at the gap between the two, and

4.   Take action to fill the gap.

If you take a look at my list, you will notice that most of the items can be achieved by me having more time and money. Some require me to improve my skills and / or my education. Others require me to have contacts and the ability to convince people to assist me in achieving my goals.

What do you need to do to 'fill the gap' so that you can achieve your goals?

_____

_____

_____

_____

_____

Now, a lot of people get to this stage and think "That's it! It's all too hard. I can't do that."

Yep, you're right.

Whatever you believe is your reality.

That's why I suggested very early in this Chapter that you forget reality. It will only discourage you (as it has been doing up to this point in your life). The facts don't count as long as you have a dream that you can become passionate about.

So, set your dreams in concrete and never get discouraged. Set plans in place to get to your dreams. If at any time things aren't working, try a different plan. Keep your dreams! Just re-plan to work your way through (or around) the challenges. Your plans should be flexible so that you can move with changing circumstances. Your dreams should be solid so that you have fixed goals to aim for.

Set your dreams in concrete and draw your plans in sand.

See the end result vividly. Feel the emotion of succeeding.

Sit quietly, close your eyes and visualise your success in full technicolour. Hear every congratulation in booming stereo. Write the script of how success will be and play the success movie in your head over and over until there is no other acceptable end result. This is your life! Plan to succeed! Never, ever give up!

Success is more often awarded for perseverance than it is awarded for talent. Talented people are everywhere. You can find them in every job, living mundane lives. It is the people with perseverance who are out there turning the world on its ear.

Much of what I have written so far requires the reader to run on faith, ignoring reality, believing in the power of their dreams. I realise that, as I write each chapter, readers are potentially turning off what I am advocating because the writings are not concerned greatly with logic and reality. However, others are already excited by the prospect of living a full exciting life and will be there at the end of the last chapter. Please be excited by the amazing prospects for your life.

I remember, many years ago, coming to the end of a Goal Setting segment within a two-day course I was running for a Coal Mine. The people in the course were not volunteers. They had been sent to the course by their employer. That's not to say that we didn't have some excellent discussions with some very intelligent, open-minded people but ...a couple of the attendees were a little less enthused than others. One particular exchange stays in my mind, with words similar to:

Attendee: "So, if I do all of this, then you're guaranteeing that everything I attempt will be successful."

Wayne: "No."

Attendee: "Then what's the point of doing all this rubbish?"

Wayne: "Because if you don't follow this process then your chance of success is significantly less. I cannot guarantee you success but I can guarantee you a better shot at success."

I don't think that he was convinced.

In fact, many people go through life not attempting any big goals because they don't want to be disappointed, should they fail. Many people are discouraged from attempting to reach their dreams because people who love them (eg parents) don't want to see them get hurt. There are even those who will discourage people from pursuing their dreams because they don't want them to succeed, not necessarily out of any conscious desire to hurt the person but through a sub-conscious rivalry. (Their sub-conscious mind is whispering "If they succeed, how bad will I look for being average?")

This is not meant as the 'Positive Bubbly Book'. People plan and work hard and still fail. Think of the most successful people that you know of. There is a good chance that they have failed many times. Successful people fail more because, quite simply, they try more.

If you look back a couple of pages at my list of goals, the second goal reads:

Have a four-wheel-drive holiday around Australia

It used to read:

Have a four-wheel-drive holiday around Australia with Loretta & Stuart.

Loretta and Stuart were Lindi's parents (my parents-in-law) - wonderful people who would, every second year, pack up their four wheel drive vehicle and caravan and travel for three or four months around and through Australia. Stuart was a loud, outgoing character and would make friends wherever he went. Loretta was lovely (the best mother-in-law in the world). I would have loved to go on a trip with them. I was busy with a family and a small business ...and they grew old and died.

I have looked back and wondered what I could have done to have made that dream come true. I couldn't. With a family and a business,

I just couldn't have afforded the time at that stage of my life. I failed at that dream.

I reset the goal.

Does failing at this goal affect my chances of success with any of my other goals? No. They are independent goals and I am still working toward my other goals.

Then again, thinking about it, maybe the answer is 'Yes'. I may have a better chance of achieving the other goals, now, because I failed at this one. I have tasted failure. I don't like the taste.

Don't be afraid of failure.

Consider the consequences of failure before you launch into your action. You will probably find that it is not such a catastrophic outcome.

Susan Jeffers, in her book *Feel the Fear and Do It Anyway* convinced me that there was no such thing as a wrong decision ...only choices with different consequences.

If you can handle the consequences of failure then why not grasp at success?

Lindi and I started our own business in 1994. At the time I was earning very good money, working in an office at a Coal Mine. I didn't have to leave. We had a mortgage and two young children. After I had submitted my notice, many of my work colleagues told me that they had considered leaving as well but 'the time wasn't right for them'. Others told me how brave (or stupid) I was to take the risk of leaving a secure, well-paid position to start up my own business.

Lindi and I had talked about the success of our plans. We had also talked about failure.

The consequence of the failure of the business was that we would sell our house and, with the left over money, buy a four wheel drive vehicle and take our children on an extended tour of Australia. Then we would come back, sell the vehicle and start again ...find another job with the same skill set and attitude that had earned me the previous well paid position and save toward another home.

Let's not dwell on the potential for failure, though. You have the potential for success. What do you want to do?

How many stars are there in the night sky?

Do you think anyone has ever counted them?

You might think "Sure, some scientist somewhere has probably plotted them and counted them."

With what technology has that scientist seen the stars? With every leap in technology, we see more stars deeper in space. How many stars still lie outside our technology's view? How large is the universe anyway?

The stars cannot be counted.

Count your potential in the same way that you count stars. Its boundaries are always outside of the range of your vision and understanding. Your potential is amazing. I am not talking to any 'chosen few' here. I am talking to everyone. Your potential is limitless. You were born with everything you need to be amazing.

You were born complete – capable of achieving anything you want to achieve.

Be successful. Live a wonderful life!

I am resilient. All challenges are temporary and are quickly overcome - nothing stops me from achieving my goals.

I have a positive expectation of success.

RELATIONSHIPS

Wouldn't it be nice to have perfect relationships – with your partner, with your children, with your parents, with your extended family, with your friends, with work colleagues ...

Wouldn't life be great!

Good relationships are at the core of life. They are core to family and they are core to business but how do you define a good, working relationship and how do you make them happen?

Many readers will probably not need to read the above words that are to them obvious. Others can be prone to believe that they don't need anyone else and that they can tell the world where to go and still be successful. It might work. It might work with a lot less pain and struggle, though, if you get on with your fellow human being.

Let's go back to basics. (When I say basics ...I, nevertheless, accept that not everyone will agree with my perception of 'basics'.) We were all born. We, our souls for want of a more definite description, came from somewhere prior to being born. In Stephen Covey's wonderful book, *The 7 Habits of Highly Successful People*, he quoted the words of Teilhard de Chardin: "We are not human beings having a spiritual experience. We are spiritual beings having a human experience." This was both an enlightenment and a comfortable fit for me as it fell in very snugly with my spiritual beliefs. The person you are having difficulty with is not behaving how you want that person to behave because he or she wasn't put on this earth to behave the way that you want them to behave.

We all, at some stage, fall into the trap of having expectations of some other person. He will meet the deadline that I set. She will be ready when it is time to leave. He will put the cap back on the toothpaste. (Divorces have occurred over that one.) She will enquire about the job advertisement that I cut out of the paper. He will put petrol in the car before he returns it to me. She will iron my shirt because she is my wife.

Iron your own shirt!!!!

We set all of these expectations and then become frustrated and angry when our expectations are not met. Want a hint for a stress-free life?

Have no expectations of anyone.

You could ask politely for something to be done. "Would you please put petrol in the car before you return it?" (And we all know that this can be said with a variety of intonations. Choose the polite, non-sarcastic, non-irritated one!) If it doesn't happen and you know that you had conveyed a clear message, then you have the right to ask (in a friendly, enquiring manner) why the petrol hasn't been topped up. You might be surprised to find that there is a logical explanation. Equally, you might be surprised that there is no good reason and your request has simply been ignored.

Ask yourself: Would I get upset about this scenario? If the answer is 'yes', now ask yourself 'why?'. Is this something that is going to have an impact on your life in five years time? ...next week?

If you were honest with yourself, you might reach into your core for the reason you are upset and find that you are upset that you didn't win that clash of wills ...You weren't on top. The other party didn't do what you told them to do.

Where did you attain the privilege to tell another soul how to behave?

By all means ask for what you want (we discussed that one earlier) but don't expect as if it were your right.

The other side (a worse side, in my opinion) of having expectations is when that expectation is met ...and you take it for granted and have no gratitude. Your partner irons your shirt for you and you put it on and don't think a thing about it. That's their job? That's their role in life? Their soul was brought into material form on this planet, in this galaxy, to iron your shirt?

When you leave the table after eating a lovely meal that has been prepared for you, do you remember to thank the person who prepared it?

I have found that when I show gratitude for what I receive, rather than have expectation of receiving something, life fills with a calm bliss.

Show gratitude for what you receive.

You might also find that when people see appreciation from you, that the task that you once expected and didn't receive will be given to you as a gift. The appreciation must be sincere, though, or the 'magic' will not work.

I rush to add that I am not a saint and I sometimes don't walk the talk. I have thrown my tantrums when I had expectations that weren't met. Life was far from blissful during those periods. (I obviously needed to have both experiences so that I could compare the two and suggest to you which was the most pleasurable.)

A principle sits at the base of this discussion: We are all individuals. View every person that you meet as a fellow spirit who is on this earth for a reason. They deserve your respect and good manners.

View every person that you meet as a fellow spirit.

We are all equal. In a family ...at work, be above no-one. Be below no-one. The Buddhists refer to this as Equanimity.

You may have noted that I mentioned 'conveyed a clear message'. So much of our angst in relationships can be attributed to poor communication. Sometimes it is just a simple misunderstanding.

No matter how much we try to communicate clearly, sometimes it will just be misunderstood. I think I have already mentioned that we all perceive a different reality – based on what we perceive through our physical senses, through our experiences, through our mental processes. All those filters between us and what is going on around us can sometimes lead to a very blurry view of what was really intended.

For this reason, we should always try to avoid sloppy communication. Sometimes when you are tired or over-stretched (trying to manage too many things at one time) it is easy to mumble something that you understand as perfectly coherent but the message ends up being totally misinterpreted by the receiver of the information. Believe me, in almost every case, it will take you longer to fix the problem than it would have taken to take a deep breath, focus the mind and clearly explain your instruction / request the first time (and then asked for feedback to ascertain that the information had been received clearly and correctly).

I have always thought it would be a good idea to put together a Mind Reading course - simply because, the next step after sloppy communication is the ridiculous assertion (usually after a disastrous event) of 'They should have known!' People who are very familiar with each other (husband and wife come to mind as an example) often fall into this trap.

An event may occur that infuriates one or the other and the other party wonders why the air is a little 'icy'. One has done something that the other doesn't like them doing. But before that person became angry, they should have asked themselves the question: "Have I ever told them that I don't like them doing that?" It is not rare that the honest answer would be "No". Divorces have happened!

Some people's life experiences have placed them in a situation where they find it very difficult to point out to another person that they don't like a particular behaviour. Some people are non-assertive to the level of 'timid'. I don't use this terminology to be demeaning. It is a serious problem that affects a large proportion of society. What makes it more difficult for them is that the other proportion of society is largely made up of people who are aggressive and are prepared to have their way at the expense of the rights of others.

The Assertive person (the one who is looking for the best result for everyone) is very rare.

I have conducted Assertiveness Courses. It is my firm opinion that everyone should attend an Assertiveness Course during their school years or as soon as possible after that time. What a wonderful society we would have if everyone knew how to talk calmly and logically (without getting angry and stressed) while working toward the perfect outcome of a discussion. What if everyone had been trained to 'respond' (listen, overcome the emotion that the statement caused, think about the perfect outcome for everyone, respond with the correct words and level of calmness to lead the discussion toward the perfect outcome) rather than 'react' (anger, yelling, emotion).

In fact, there are two things, which relate to this chapter, that I have been a little pushy about in my life. The first is my conviction that everyone should take part in an Assertiveness Course.

Enrol in an Assertiveness Course.

The second is (and this seems so fundamental to me) to get to know who you are sharing your planet with ...through to the level of knowing who you are sharing your house with. (And you think to yourself: "Yes Wayne. I have met everyone in my house".) Meeting them is not what I mean. Knowing how they will behave during a discussion or negotiation or under stress is what I mean.

Everyone has a combination of personality types that have their own set of personality traits that are both positive (good for the world) and negative (not so good for the world). Knowing what personality traits people have been born with will enable you to understand the best means of communicating with those people and gaining a good outcome from discussions.

Even better, if the other people know their personality traits, they can develop the positive traits and work on downgrading the negative traits.

I read a book on this (fundamental) subject and I have been a little pushy in wanting other people to read it. Most don't consider it important and don't read it. I don't understand this! (Later, we will discuss the exhilaration of the knowledge that we don't have to understand.)

This could make a huge difference in your life. I highly recommend that you read:

Recommended Reading:
Personality Plus
(Florence Littauer).

The knowledge gained from this book has made a huge difference in my life! Enough said. I'll move on before I start to sound 'pushy'.

Another impediment to good relationships is the terrible habit that many human beings have of criticising other human beings. I believe that this originates from low self-esteem. We feel better (higher up the chain) if we are putting someone else down. This terrible habit of criticising others has at least two undesirable outcomes:

1. The person that is being criticized may find out. This damages a relationship.

2. The person that is listening to the criticism thinks to themselves "I wonder what they say about me when I'm not in the room?" This damages a relationship.

There is an old adage that is so old and has been used so often that it has lost a great deal of its power. That doesn't make it any the less true.

If you cannot say anything nice about someone, say nothing at all.

I once heard someone extend this adage:

If you cannot say anything nice about someone, think harder.

It would be a very poor example of a human being if you honestly couldn't think of one good trait to comment on rather than the criticism that you were about to make. Everyone has faults. Everyone has good points. We are all human beings. Common respect (and a desire for good relationships) dictates that we should do our best not to criticise for the sake of criticism.

Having said this, I will hurriedly add that there are times for discussion of another person's strengths and weaknesses. I have met people who have taken the above adage to the extreme of not discussing anything about another person. When you are part of a team that needs to work together to perform and meet outcomes (eg work, service clubs), then it is important to be able to discuss fellow members (but here's the difference) with the intention of putting actions in place to assist them to develop and become a better team contributor.

The point at hand is for a person not to put themselves in the position of judge of their fellow human beings. That role belongs to a higher being and that being is polite enough, I hear, to wait until the end of the game (life) before giving a verdict.

Some other simple (but not necessarily easy) things to do to promote good relationships:

1. Have no anger.
    I know this isn't easy. My father had a spontaneous temper. He was a wonderful, loving man but he could just erupt verbally ...and then apologise very soon after. I learned that same, sudden temper. It took years to overcome and I can still slip on the very rare occasion.

However, if the aim is wonderful relationships, then there is no room for temper. Respond. Do not 'React'.

2. Disconnect the Buttons.
    All of us have that thing that annoys us. That button that causes us to go wild when someone pushes it.

    "It drives me crazy when he …", "I just explode every time she …".

    We could spend a lot of time wondering why you react that way. (You will notice that I used the word 'react'.) Whether that 'wondering time' would be time well spent is another question.

    The solution is to just stop reacting. Easier said than done, of course. Necessary, nevertheless.

    Would it help you if I told you that, by owning these buttons, you have given other people power over your life. You've given someone the ability to turn your life from good to rotten in a fraction of a second, just by pressing your (well advertised) button.

    Some of the people who have pressed your button probably walk away with a smile on their lips. Wouldn't it feel better if you maintained your good mood and they walked away confused? (Before I became a little more enlightened, I used to say "Love your Enemy. It drives them nuts!".)

    Others, who have inadvertently touched the button, walk away hurt and the relationship is damaged as a result.

Recognise your buttons (They tend to be pretty obvious.) and then disconnect them - by working on calmly responding rather than reacting. Relationships will change for the better.

3. Serve.
    I heard somewhere, but don't remember where or from whom (which is disappointing to me because when I know a source, I prefer to give credit) that "If you want to be Master of the World, then Serve your fellow man." I don't want to be Master of the World and I don't think many sensible people would but I did run a very successful business for almost two decades and it was based on giving service to other business people who became my friends. There is no great pain in providing service to your friends, ...in assisting them to achieve their objectives. People with an incorrect ego setting will not find it easy but relationships flourish for the person with a controlled ego.

4. Accept everyone.
    I love the beautiful Buddhist principle of Equanimity. Everyone is my equal.

    Every person is a soul in human form. They have faults, no doubt. I have faults, no doubt. No-one is greater than me. No-one is less than me. We are all souls on earth with a mission.

5. Talk Positively.
    I cannot talk for other cultures but in Australia sarcasm reigns supreme. You've got to be tough to grow up in some families. You've go to be tough to go through an

apprenticeship. It is considered fun and good natured to put others down and to give them 'a hard time'.

It's all done in good spirit and with the best of humorous intention. If only those people really understood the damage that they were doing to those young people ...to their own children. Self-image and confidence are so easily damaged.

This negative put-down is so much the Australian culture that I developed Affirmations to remind myself not to fall into this horrible habit:

Affirmations:

My 'talk' to my family, friends and associates is always positive and encouraging. My sphere of influence is in peace and harmony.

Everything I do and say leads to the improved self-image of my family members and the people around me.

Another book that I found to contain wonderful relationship information is:

Recommended Reading:
Real Magic
(Dr Wayne Dyer).

In the end, after all your wonderful efforts to develop spectacular relationships throughout all facets of your life, something will occasionally happen where you are left not understanding the behaviour of someone. You did everything you could and the relationship still went through a bumpy patch. You stand back, scratch your head and with furrowed brow you exclaim, "I don't understand."

So, ...why do you think you will understand everything? Why do you need to understand? Human relationships are a complex thing. This next piece of advice was very liberating for me. It un-furrowed my brow on many more topics that just relationships.

You don't have to understand.

You might notice that this Chapter on Relationships is almost at an end and you might think "Hang on. You haven't spent much time discussing the Relationship between a man and woman who are trying to share the same household and trying to manage a budget and trying to raise children and ... What about some specific information on that topic? Help!"

Too many good books have already been written on that subject for me to try to add my little bit in this condensed book. Suffice to say that everything I have written in this Chapter is applicable to that very important Relationship but for more information I refer you to some brilliant books that I highly recommend:

Recommended Reading:
Men Are From Mars, Women Are From Venus
(John Gray Ph.D.)

**Recommended Reading:
His Needs Her Needs
(Willard F. Harley, Jr.)**

**Recommended Reading:
The Five Love Languages
(Gary Chapman).**

Now, I want to be able to write a practical book. I know that many people are going to think, occasionally, during this book that 'Wayne is on something'. It wouldn't be the first time that I've heard 'Wayne's World' uttered. There are obviously failed relationships in this world. I am not going to be so positive minded and impractical to ignore the fact that some relationships should not be continued. Having said that, I obviously haven't the skillset or knowledge of anyone's circumstance that I can make suggestions.

I simply want to end this Chapter making it clear to everyone that, regardless of everything I've written about the skills of having wonderful relationships, that no-one should feel bad / judged for having to end a relationship. That too takes courage.

HEALTH

I have no medical qualifications. I cannot produce a University Degree or any other written form that will convince you to listen to what I believe.

I do, however, have an asset that may give me some credence. Like you, I am the proud owner of a Human Body.

The Human Body is an amazing, complex creation. It would take more than a couple of University Degrees to understand the full complexity of its operation …if, indeed, modern science did possess all of that information. The best way to look after it is a matter of conjecture and argument. It came without a User's Manual. For every number of experts who tells you to do one thing, you will find a similar number of experts who want to tell you to do something contradictory. Some of these 'experts' represent vested interests. The rest just disagree!

A friend recently suffered some illness and went through a round of Doctors and Specialists. She tries to stay healthy. She tries to keep up a good intake of water. She fails, as most of us do, to drink as much as the experts suggest. (I've read that it should be about eight glasses of water a day.) If we all drank as much as the experts suggest, we would spend a large part of our day walking to and from the toilet. I know that I have never been able to consistently drink my quota. Neither has my friend. A Specialist Doctor told her to **reduce** her intake of water! Conflicting ideas from the experts!

I take supplements. By that I mean Vitamin Tablets. A lot of experts suggest that Supplement intake is a good way to enhance our diet based on the fact that we don't always eat the right foods and even the right foods aren't necessarily the quality source that they used to be. Some of these experts represent the Companies that make the Vitamin Tablets. Many don't, however, have a vested interest. My Family Doctor, without having articulated his opinion in so many words, is obviously of the school of thought that Vitamins are a waste of money and just make for expensive urine. Who do you believe?

I have a good idea of who you should believe. You are the prime expert on your body. I think that YOU know what is best for YOUR body. I also think that the vast majority of you know that you are not doing what is best for your body.

Many years ago, I developed an Atopic Heart Beat. I think it was associated with the high level of stress causers in my life. (I refuse to react with stress any more.) Simply put, my heart was missing beats. Missing the beat wasn't the main problem. During a missed beat, the heart continues to fill with blood so that the next beat has to be bigger to move the extra blood and is like someone knocking on your chest. Try to get to sleep at night with that going on!

The doctor did his tests and confirmed his diagnosis. I asked what we should do. He told me that the drugs had terrible side effects and he didn't recommend them. He told me that an operation to disconnect the faulty part of the heart's electric circuit was probably not necessary in my case. He told me to live with it and taught me a technique of holding my breath.

I take responsibility for the health of my body.

Some time later, I went to a Health Conference. One of the speakers was talking on the value of Vitamin Supplements. She rattled through a list of Vitamins and Minerals and listed what areas of the body they were good for. I cannot remember anything she listed after she said "…and Calcium is good for regulating heart beat". I went home and took a serious interest in ensuring that I swallowed Calcium Magnesium tablets every day. Within three weeks the Atopic Heart Beat had disappeared. As long as I take the tablets regularly, the Atopic Heart Beat stays away. You wouldn't think anyone would be dumb enough to get slack about taking tablets that provide such an obvious health benefit, would you? When I get slack and don't take the tablets regularly, the Atopic Heart Beat returns.

The point of the example is …Who is really the expert? Ask Yourself: "Who has the greatest vested interest in my health?"

The best way to keep a body healthy is actually just common sense. (Yes, we've all been told that common sense isn't common. I find that negative and insulting to the majority of my fellow space travelers. Moving on.) However, in the hectic world in which we live, trying to find a balance in all the areas of our lives often means that looking after our body doesn't rate at the high-end of our priority list. Why is this? I think it is because our bodies are so forgiving. We can neglect it and neglect it and it still continues to function …albeit with some minor noises and aches. However, one day we will find ourselves in a state of illness.

I remember being in an office talking to a friend who was obviously depressed. His wife had just been diagnosed with a degenerative disease. I don't know how well she was looking after her health. We live in a time when air, food and water are full of toxins. Regardless of our best efforts, disease can still happen. (We still need to give our best effort, though, to give ourselves the best chance.)

It wasn't the cause of the disease that interested me. It was the impact on lives. This man was quite healthy for his age. He was close to retirement. He and his wife had wonderful plans for what they would do when he retired, …with all the years of work behind them. Those plans were in tatters! The future wasn't going to be the great adventure that they had planned and that they had worked so hard for over all of those years.

Your health is Extremely Important.
(And not just to you.)

You've probably noticed, with your reading so far, that I like to get back to the basics. So …getting back to basics, *what is a Human Body?*

If you accept my unsubstantiated belief that your soul has taken residence in your human body, then that makes the human body like a space suit.

We are on a planet with an atmosphere that contains mainly Oxygen. Our space suit has, therefore, been designed to draw in the atmosphere and extract the Oxygen that can be used to provide the power for the reactions that are necessary to maintain the space suit.

Our space suit has been designed to ingest solids and fluids that will be used to provide the power to move the suit at our beckoning. Further, this causes waste products that can be eliminated, by clever design, from our space suit.

This suit is a very complex and wonderful apparatus. If you needed proof that it should have come with a User's Manual, then ask a six month old baby to go out and hunt down some food. The child will only stare (or cry) at you. That child is still trying to work out how to grab things and roll off its back. It cannot walk and it is still trying to work out what the hell you are talking about.

Imagine that you are an Astronaut and you've just landed on the moon. Suited up in your Astronaut space suit, you leave your landing craft and start teaching yourself how to move in this new environment. One of the main purposes of your suit is to provide you with Oxygen. How is your imagination? I can imagine myself into a claustrophobic condition. Walking on the moon with my life dependent on a piece of material to keep in the Oxygen that is keeping me alive. How keen would you be to look after that suit? Would you run the risk of tearing it or puncturing it?

Why is our personal on-earth space suit (our Human Body) of less importance? I think that it just comes down to familiarity. We have had our bodies since we were born and we, incorrectly, see it as us.

My Human Body is not me. It is my Soul's Space Suit.

So, regardless of whether you accept my unsubstantiated belief or not, we should be able to agree that it is important to look after your body. Of course it has a used-by-date and will one day stop working and simply give up its ability to support life. But, up to that date, wouldn't it be wonderful if it operated to its full effectiveness in all of its operational requirements.

(The Manufacturers Warranty is Null and Void if the purchased item is found to have been abused.)

So, we've discussed what the body is and how important it is to keep it well maintained …and the fact that you (as your body's expert) already know the best things to do for it. Now all we need is a commitment from you to give your body a higher priority.

Looking after the health of my body is a top priority.

IMPORTANT INFORMATION:
Don't kill yourself getting healthy.
Talk to your Doctor if you are in any doubt about how any of these suggestions may affect your individual needs.

Presuming that we are starting with a relatively healthy body, let's look at some of the ways of looking after it …that you already know:

1   Exercise.
     Your body is designed to move. Our modern lifestyle has led us to become too sedentary. I'm not talking about taking out a Gym membership, running marathons or buying any specialised equipment. Just move.

     Walking two or three times a week (say for half an hour each time) will make a wonderful difference. Be defensive about it. Don't walk in areas that are not safe. Don't walk at night. If you prefer to walk at night, then at least get some high visibility clothes. (I drive past people at night who are walking the road, wearing black! That's not healthy!)

     If you don't like walking then find a physical activity that you like. In fact, its better to get your exercise from something that you enjoy because that means that exercise is fun rather than a chore. Dancing? Skating? Social Tennis? What would you like to do?

2   Eat Well.
     We all know that most Take-Away food and all food that is full of fat and sugar is going to store fat in our body and

fill the arteries with cloggy stuff that can eventually lead to a heart attack. But it tastes good, doesn't it?

I'm not a health nut. I like the occasional hamburger and packet of chips. I'm a savory person. Other people are sugar people – cakes, chocolate …

Everything in moderation!

Cut those items down to a once in a while treat. Increase your intake of steamed vegetables. Reduce the amount of meat that you put on your plate. Some experts suggest a piece of meat the size of the palm of your hand (no counting the fingers!) and then the rest of the plate should be vegetables. You already know all this. It's just that the pace of life gets in the way!

I'm not suggesting a diet. I am suggesting a permanent change in lifestyle.

3   Change your habits.
Bad habits that you know need changing are:

A. Excessive alcohol intake,
B. Taking social drugs,
C. Excessive coffee intake,
D. Smoking,
E. Reacting stressfully to situations,
F. Driving like a maniac (just thought I'd throw that one in),
G. Others that I won't mention here. (You know if you have unhealthy habits. Remove them from your life.)

4   Meditate.

Why have I included Meditation here? Because while we are talking health, we should also discuss mental health. There has, in the past, been a stigma attached to various forms of mental illness and I hope that the stigma is disappearing.

Mental illness is an illness of the body like any other illness. It has its effects on the body and, after a period of being treated, the body has the potential to return to full health.

The number of people that I know who suffer Depression and other forms of mental illness is alarming. The number of young people that I know who are on medication for mental problems is alarming.

I'm not suggesting Meditation as a cure. I'm just suggesting that everyone should give their mind a break. This is a very hectic time in history. Your mind is always busy, always under attack from a magnificent array of inputs and stress causers. Even while you sleep, the mind is working on the problems that you need solutions for. Scenarios are being run through your mind as dreams and nightmares.

Take time (even if it's only five minutes) to sit quietly and let your mind relax. Meditation doesn't have to be about stopping the mind from thinking. Even if you just took it to a nice place ...somewhere you enjoyed during your childhood. Give it some nice thoughts. Give it a short holiday.

I don't think that I've told you any great revelation regarding how to look after your body. You know it all. If you're like me, then you just aren't giving it enough of a priority. I'm not exercising enough. My nutritional intake, I think, is pretty good. And I have the 'bad habits' area under control.

What does this mean? I need to give more priority to exercise! That's honest. You, too, need to be honest about your health program.

When we talked about Balance in Chapter 3, we looked at the old plan of:

Review, Change, Find the Balance, Repeat the process.

Health is one of the factors in that Life Balance exercise. The principle of continually reviewing your health and making changes to your activity to get back to a Health Balance is fundamental to your continued enjoyment of life …and, ultimately, your continued habitation of your space suit!

AND …this isn't just about you! If you abuse your body and die, then you're dead. So isn't that just the ultimate result of living on earth? But what about the people that you, untimely, leave behind?

I had an Uncle who I didn't meet. He became an alcoholic, never married, didn't associate with family, lived to be an old, unhappy man and then died. Question: What caused this? Answer: His mother (a very large, unfit lady) died of a heart attack when he was a teenager. He simply didn't get over the grief.

Are you someone's Mother? Father? Grandparent? What effect will it have on the child who absolutely adores you, if you suddenly aren't there anymore …just because you didn't look after your health? What will it do to your loving partner to be left without you?

Health Affirmation:

**I am a very healthy person.
I enjoy abundance in health.**

WEALTH / PROSPERITY

Let's clear the air right up front. In this Chapter, I'm not talking about Abundance – where we have to define the term and talk about Abundance in Relationships and Abundance in Health and how much more important they are than just plain money.

I can move past that because we have already given those subjects their own Chapters and talked about how important they are. We've talked about Balance.

Now, I am talking about Money!

In this Chapter, it is obviously not my intention to discuss investment options. I am not a Financial Adviser. I am not familiar with the Investment Potential in your part of the world. Most importantly, this book will age. I am very confident that a process of investment that suits one generation of investors may be totally inappropriate a small number of years later. I am also very aware of the differences between countries and between areas of a country of the likely returns on the same type of investment.

My aim with this Chapter is to highlight the need to understand your attitude to money and to start the process of putting money together so that you can begin being an investor and begin working toward a wealthy lifestyle.

Nobody highlighted this for me when I was young! It has only been in the latter part of my life that I have really started to learn. Books are important, as are successful people who you are prepared to learn from. I now have, I believe, a very good and balanced attitude toward money.

There are many people in this world who have disgusting attitudes to money. Their attitudes might be 'disgusting' based on the way they need money and will do anything to get it. Or their attitudes might be 'disgusting' based on their purity in believing that anyone who has money is a bad person.

I once had a lady explain to me that anyone who had money was a crook. Amazing! What do you think her chances are of ever being anything other than what Australian's call a 'battler'. (ie Someone who battles …struggles to pay the bills and rake together a living.)

Let's talk about Money and then we'll discuss the poor attitudes.

Money is a thing. It is neither good nor bad. What people do with it can be good or bad. People's behaviour toward money can be good or bad. But …money is a neutral thing.

Money will often reveal the true nature of the person who possesses it.

No, Money is not everything …but it is up there with Oxygen and is way ahead of whatever commodity comes next.

Money may not be able to buy happiness …but most people will be pretty miserable (and hungry) without it.

Money is a means of exchange. You can buy health cover and, therefore, give yourself and your family a better chance of returning to good health from sickness. You can donate to charities and assist people less fortunate than yourself. You can pay more taxes and, therefore, put more into Community.

Let's not forget this one: You can buy things for yourself and your loved ones and, therefore, keep the economy rolling over so that people will have jobs in manufacturing, sales and service industries.

How's your attitude toward money? Are you in one of the extreme groups? Are you prepared to do anything to get money? Are you proud of yourself for being a good person – for not having money?

Let me tell you where I sit: I would like to be wealthy so that I can live a life without having to worry about whether I have the money to pay the bills and without having to look at my bank balance to decide whether or not to do something that I want to do. I would like to have the money to donate to assist causes that I want to assist.

Is there anything evil in that statement? Wouldn't that be a good beginning as a start toward living a wonderful life?

Yes, relationships, health and other things that we discussed and are yet to discuss will come into play to determine whether life will indeed be wonderful ...but having financial wealth will weigh the balance a little more toward the possibility of 'wonderful'.

I've had people say to me: "I don't want to be a millionaire. I just want to be comfortable." Have you heard that one? Have you said it? Why not be a millionaire *and* be comfortable. (You may want to consider having more than a million. A million doesn't buy as much as it once did.)

Have you considered how good it would be for your country if you had lots of money. Stop being so selfish in refusing the money and start thinking about the health of your nation! If you love your country, get rich. Pay more taxes. Buy more things. Get your economy moving. One of the greatest things that a population can do for their country is to be wealthy.

Why do people think it is bad to have money?

1. Family Education.
    Attitudes to money are often bred at home and are passed
    from generation to generation.

    In Australia, I can see the effects of our Colonial history
    and the class structure of that period. There were the poor
    and the rich and a huge distrust between.

    Early in the Twentieth Century, there was the Great
    Depression that left a financial scar on most working class
    families. Not having money, if nothing else, provided a
    badge of honour for being part of the community that
    helped each other through. It led to a pride in being
    working class and without money.

2. The Rich Behaving Badly.
    The people who will do anything to get money (even after
    they have more than sufficient) have a bad attitude to
    money (as we've already discussed). When these people
    fall, they usually fall very visually.

    There are a multitude of examples of the rich being
    visually greedy and opposed to community values and
    being dragged through the courts. People without money
    see this as further evidence of the corrupt properties of
    money and, sometimes, as vindication of their correct
    choice to be poor.

    The far greater number of good, wealthy people who are
    going about their lives and making a contribution to their
    families and friends and charities are not seen and the

visual, bad display of greedy wealth becomes the image of all wealthy people.

3.   They don't have money.
        People, very generally speaking, blame set. When something goes wrong in their lives, they look for someone else to blame. When they are not as successful as someone else then they look to allocate blame elsewhere.

        When someone has money and someone else doesn't, that makes the person without money look wrong. Have they been lazy? Have they not had enough intelligence?

        That's when it becomes very easy to drag out the old chestnuts: "They must be crooks", "Ahh, but they won't get into heaven", "Money is the root of all evil", "I bet they're not happy".

4.   People are Envious.
        When one person is successful in a particular area (eg Wealth) and another is not, it is all too easy to quietly slander the successful person – motivated by a combination of envy and the points above.

Important Note: If you find yourself having problems with what I am writing in this Chapter, I refer you to more specific books on Money. (See the Recommended Reading as we work through this Chapter and at the end of the book.) I apologise if my approach has not suited you …but there are many good books on Money for your review.

Now that we have discussed attitudes to Wealth, let's talk about becoming wealthy.

I once tried to explain the process of becoming wealthy to a young man who thought it was about betting on horses. I tried to put the process in very simple terms for him:

Spend more than you earn and you will be poor.

Spend less than you earn and you will be wealthy.

This led to the next problem. He knew how much he earned but he had no idea how much he spent.

This is not a rare problem!

Do you have a budget of your income and expenditure? It needs to be all encompassing (preferably over a year) so that there are no sudden surprises. ("Oh, I forgot about repairs to the car. That will knock the budget around.")

Prepare an all-encompassing Budget.

Don't be too hard on yourself during this budgeting process. You need to enjoy life or you are going to 'break out' and blow the budget and then give up. Allow for entertainment – within your means.

The next step after going to the not-too-small an effort of producing a Budget is to actually stick to it.

Once a sensible budget is in place, the Income is not of interest and the Expenditure is not of interest. (If you can increase the Income and / or decrease the Expenditure, then this is, of course, a good time to do so.) What is of supreme interest is the Difference between these – the amount that can be saved and, eventually, invested.

Don't be discouraged at this point. Most people (particularly young people just starting on their financial journey) come to a Budget with debts that need to be cleared before there can be savings.

A very good book to read on this subject is:

Recommended Reading:
The Richest Man in Babylon
(George S. Clason).

There is also a very good section on Wealth and attitudes to wealth in a book that I have previously recommended:

Recommended Reading:
Real Magic
(Dr Wayne Dyer).

The aim of the budget is to get yourself to a point where you have money put aside that you can invest.

When I talk of putting money aside to invest, though, I do mean 'invest'. So many people develop that nest egg that could help them create a wealthy lifestyle and then decide that it would be nice to use their 'savings' for a really nice holiday or a new car. "After all," they say "I've saved hard. I deserve a reward."

You deserve to be wealthy ...and then you can go on many holidays and buy 'toys' ...and help others.

A wealthy lifestyle rarely happens overnight. Develop patience! Lack of patience can lead to 'broke'.

Before I leave this topic, I will share with you some strategies that I have been using on my financial path. I offer them for your consideration:

1.   Understand an Asset and a Liability.
     An asset is something that will earn you money. A Liability is something that will cost you money. I'm not sure what the Accounting Textbooks say, but that's my understanding ...in a nutshell.

     That means the Home in which you live is not an Asset. A car is not an Asset. A recreational boat is not an Asset

     Robert Kiyosaki put a different slant on things when he defined an Asset as something that will feed you and a Liability as something that will eat you.

2.   Keep your overheads low.
     When things are tough (as they tend to be on a cyclic basis), it is good not to have Creditors knocking on your door. It's good to be still able to pay your bills.

Just on that subject, I have seen so many young people get their first job and rush out to go into debt over a brand new car.

In my mid-fifties, I, personally, have never owned a new car. My businesses have owned some new little hatchbacks over the years but I have never bought that new, expensive car. When you do see me driving *that* car, you will know that I have too much money and I couldn't think of anything else to do with it.

3. Keep the Ego in check.
    When things are going well, it's easy to get carried away with yourself. The universe has ways of keeping your ego in check if you don't seem to be able to manage it for yourself.

    In the good times and the bad times, people have always known where they stood with me …because who I was didn't change with the times.

4. Take charge of your finances.
    Too many people hand the management of their finances over to someone else ('the expert'). Quite apart from the worry of being defrauded, consider that no-one else cares as much about your financial security as you do. Your finances should be yours to manage.

    Taking charge also means educating yourself and keeping abreast of financial matters.

5.	Make Sensible, Considered Decisions.
	I like Warren Buffett's approach to investing. I have read in Financial Papers that his rule one is "Don't loose money" and that his rule two is "Remember Rule One".

	Don't rush in. Don't rely on your sixth sense, on gut feeling or on luck until after you have done your research.

6.	Diversify.
	As soon as it is possible, spread your risk over a number of different investment areas.

	"Don't put all your eggs in the one basket", is the old wisdom.

7.	Consider your own circumstances before taking advice.
	By all means, listen ...but don't buy in unless it suits your individual needs.

	Even this book! You have your own particular needs that someone giving advice cannot understand.

	Investment is the same. You are unique. Listen well. Take action on advice cautiously.

8.	Look for a Passive Income.
	An active income is one where you are putting in effort for every unit of return on investment. (eg A Tradesman working for an hourly rate.) Someone with an active income has to be there, working away, or the money stops.

A passive income is where money is dropping into your bank account while you are away on a holiday. (eg Rental Property.)

Recommended Reading:
Rich Dad, Poor Dad
(Robert T. Kiyosaki).

Recommended Reading:
Cashflow Quadrant
(Robert T. Kiyosaki).

I have been honest with you, during the writing of this book. On occasion, I have opened my heart for view. I have stated clearly that, in this book, I am occasionally the example of 'getting it wrong'. I am just another person trying to find his course through life and I am definitely not the guru on any subject.

I will not finish this Chapter without confirming my message on the first page of this Chapter. I don't want you to be under any delusion that I am a wealthy man telling you how he got rich.

Nobody highlighted this for me when I was young! It has only been in the latter part of my life that I have really started to learn.

I have made many financial mistakes and lived a large part of my life in financial ignorance but great changes have occurred since I have been applying what I have written here.

I hope that what I have written kindles, within you, an interest to know more and to develop. Read the recommended Books if you are truly seeking guidance. I wish you Wealth.

Affirmation:

I am a very successful person with affluence in money and affluence in all other areas of life. My family's lifestyle is admired by those around us.

MAKING A DIFFERENCE

When you saw the title of this Chapter, you may have started working through the Catalogue System in your brain, searching for the names of people who have made a difference.

Names come to mind: Mother Teresa, Mahatma Gandhi, Winston Churchill, Abraham Lincoln, Nelson Mandela … I'm sure that you could list many more.

These people have indeed made a difference and have gone down in the history books to be remembered for generations to come …perhaps for as long as mankind survives.

You could do that too! You could become the leader of your country. You could perform any of an astounding multitude of things that would put you up there among world leaders with your name recorded for posterity.

How did you go on that little test? When you read that last paragraph, did that negative little person in your head scoff at the suggestion and say something like "Oh yeah. Of course you can" in a sarcastic little voice? Did you even react physically with an exhaust of air through your nose – as if to say "Yeah right. Who are you kidding?"

Why not? What made those people so different to you? They were born like you. They lived in a country at a particular time in history just like you are doing. They had parents and grew up and did things – just like you. What difference do you see between those people and you that you believe that they could do wonderful things but you cannot?

If you did have the sarcastic voice in your head when you read the earlier paragraph, then I can tell you one difference – they had A Mind to Achieve.

You may have already noticed that there are two meanings to the title of this book that are both applicable to these famous people who made a difference:

1.   They had a desire / plan / intention to Achieve.

2.   They had a mind / brain that was confident / supportive of their intention to Achieve.

(Why haven't you got that?)

That is not to say that they naturally had supportive minds. I'm not saying that the negative voice didn't chirp in. Indeed, Winston Churchill suffered from what he described as the 'Black Dog'. He suffered from Depression. What I am saying is that they entered into the struggle to control their minds. They trained their minds to support them. They fought the battle of their lives – inside their heads – so that the external battles could be won.

They were aware of the negative voice that opposed their confidence to succeed. Are you aware of your negative voice? Before you can combat it, you have to know it is there and you have to know what it is saying to you.

Whenever you are about to do something that is outside of your normal feeling of comfort (and I hope that you are doing that often), listen for the voice, feel your bodies reaction. Are you being told that you cannot do this? Is your mind playing videos of all the times that you failed, felt foolish or embarrassed? Are you sick in the stomach?

Are your knees turning to jelly? These reactions are all normal. We all have them – including the people that we read about in our history books. The trick is to recognise what is happening in your mind and to your body.

Now, before I go any further, I want to make it clear that you don't have to be another Winston Churchill or Mother Teresa or any other famous person that you might be thinking of. They made a very visible contribution to this world. Most people don't do things at that level and, even more importantly, don't want to do things at that level.

I do want you to get yourself to a point, though, where you know that you could operate at that level if you had the drive to do so.

The fact is that most of us don't want to be world leaders or world beaters. (If you do, then go for it!) Most of us want to lead a balanced life that has meaning – and part of that 'meaning' is to make a difference at some level.

When you look at the famous, world-changing people that we originally thought of when we looked at the title of this Chapter, we can see that they probably didn't have a very well balanced life (in the way that most of us would perceive as 'balance'). They were very focused. Their Health and Relationships might have suffered while they were focused on their goals. I can think of some who spent large sections of their lives incarcerated by their society. Twenty Seven years in Nelson Mandela's case. I cannot imagine anyone I know who would volunteer for that. Certainly not me!

My first suggestion, for finding out what your inner voice is all about, is to do something new (that is safe). I joined a Toastmasters Club. I had to be 'dragged along' by a friend because I couldn't imagine that it would be a fun experience.

Toastmasters is a wonderful organisation that provides people with the opportunity to grow (get out of their comfort zone and tame the inner voice) by placing them into a very supportive environment to learn how to deliver speeches in front of a group.

As it turned out, it was a wonderful experience – but I still remember the stress and my heart beating loudly in my ears and my stomach churning as I stood up to second a motion. "I second that motion" caused so much discomfort in my body. I had found my inner voice and it was not very supportive. It reminded me of all my failures and all my embarrassing moments.

I went on to become President of the club and spent over a decade helping others to find their inner voice and tame it. It was a great experience. Overcoming this obstacle, led me into developing and presenting training courses and that led me to acting on stage and, later, acting in front of a camera. None of this would have been possible without those early steps of discovering my negative inner voice and taking action to confront it and turn it into a supportive voice.

During those Toastmaster days, I had a mantra (Affirmation) that I would use as I walked to the lectern to present my speech. It was my three Cs. I would repeat over and over in my mind "I am Cool. I am Calm. I am Confident". This affirmation is applicable in most circumstances and I have used it in many situations to overcome and still the negative inner voice.

I am Cool. I am Calm. I am Confident

You will have seen Affirmations throughout this book. An Affirmation is a statement of what you want, expressed as if it already exists. Everyone should have a small list of Affirmations devoted to the areas that they want to work on – and they should be recited daily (more than once) so that the mind has an alternate opinion to the negative inner voice. Just a warning – initially the mind will reply with something like "that's garbage" but, with persistence and repetition you will eventually make changes.

So, you've read this book (thus far). You've looked at the Suggested Reading that I've pointed you to and maybe even dipped into a couple of those brilliant books. You know about your Negative Inner Voice and you have the knowledge to write and recite (out loud, where appropriate) your own Affirmations or the Affirmations provided in this book.

If you knew you couldn't fail, what would you do with your life?

How do you want your life to be?

What do you want to do to make a difference?

Your 'making a difference' might be to improve the relationships within your family …to do something for somebody who needs help …to work on a project within your community …to …

I don't know what your 'making a difference' is. I only know that you need to have a desire to do it AND you need to develop your mind so that it will assist you (rather than work against you) in the process.

You need A Mind to Achieve!

If you would like to make a difference, then don't let yourself be stopped by a mind that is not supportive. Take up the battle and overcome the programming that has caused the negative inner talk.

It won't be easy!

For however many years you have been on this planet your mind has been trained to react the way it does. Whether that was because of past failures, bad experiences or embarrassments or because of the negative talk that you were given as a child (I cringe when I hear parents saying things like "Your stupid" to their child), it will take some time to change that programming.

Importantly too: If you are still receiving negative input from people in your life, then you should consider avoiding those people while you are strengthening your positive mind. If they are 'friends' then maybe you should consider whether they are really good influences in your life. (At the very least, lend them this book and see if that helps.) If they are still negative, avoid them at least until your mind is stronger. If you *know* that they will not support you, then keep your process and this book secret – rather than give them an extra opportunity to give you negative input.

Once you develop a Mind to Achieve, the possibilities are limitless. You can live a magnificent life!

Go for it!

WITH SPIRIT

Wow! Hear we are at the last Chapter.

Congratulations on working your way through this book. There may have been times when you've thought about putting it aside. There would have been many other demands on your time, I'm sure.

Thank you for being at this point. I hope that it makes a significant, positive difference to your life.

This Chapter may be the most challenging. (For some.) I don't mean to sound arrogant. There are many people with greater understanding than I ...and those people may have whisked through this book thinking "When am I going to learn something new?"

We are all at different stages on our life path and life learning. I sometimes despair at how much I have to learn and how much I want to achieve ...and how little time I may have to do it all in. Others may feel comfortably on track.

As I have stated through this book, I belong to no particular religion. I was brought up in a Western Society. (Australia is geographically in the East, as it turns out, but let's not complicate the matter. How do you have East and West on a globe anyway???)

Moving on.

I have grown up in a multicultural society that, during my early years at least, was predominately considered to be a Christian society. A small number of people that I have met have 'hang-ups' about the Good or Evil of Spiritual Experiences that they consider may be

'Psychic' or 'Witchy'. So, I mean no offence to anyone by recounting the following stories. I do relate them for a purpose which I will explain later. These events happened to me when I was in my twenties (last Century!).

STORY ONE

I was sick! I had the full-on Flu. Fever, Aching Joints, Chills. I wasn't able to get out of bed for days other than occasionally struggling to walk to the toilet.

This was probably about five years after I had left school – so I would have been around twenty three years of age.

Lindi and I were both members of the State Emergency Service and we had a major exercise the following weekend – involving a mock disaster with multiple injuries and in conjunction with the Emergency Response Teams from the Police, Fire Brigade and Military (Air Force and Army). The exercise was being organised outside of our area so I was not directly involved but I had been invited along as an 'observer'. Lindi (as a Casualty Simulation Person) and our Rescue Team had been invited to participate.

I was really keen to get better so that I could observe the exercise …and, of course, so that I could stop feeling so lousy.

Fortunately, my health was improving …albeit slowly.

During my fevered sleep, I had a dream. I don't know if you have ever experienced the 'difference' in a style of dream. Some dreams, you wake up and you cannot remember what you were dreaming about. Others, you wake up and you think "that was a weird dream" and others you think "that felt entirely different to a dream and it felt more like a prediction".

The really definite part of the dream – that I remembered with total clarity – was that I was at a party. There was a person in a wheel chair. That person couldn't walk. When I walked over, I realised that it was someone that I had gone to high school with. I hadn't seen this person since leaving school and, while at school, we were in the same year but we were not in the same group.

There was no reason why I would dream about this person and, if I were to make a list of people from my school days that I may have put into a dream, there would have been dozens of names I would have mentioned and I probably wouldn't have even thought to list this person.

That was the extent of the dream. It was clear and I remembered it perfectly when I woke …and it was just as clear the next morning. It was so clear that it played on my mind. The message – a particular person, who I went to school with, could no longer walk. The 'feel' was that he had been involved in some sort of accident.

The flu had passed by the weekend and I felt well enough to observe the exercise. Lindi and I drove about half an hour away and turned our little, yellow Leyland Mini down a bush track.

We were getting close to the river when we saw our Rescue Team and they saw us. In the midst of the waving, I lost concentration (I had been sick, after all) and managed to hang the Mini up on its sump on the centre mound of dirt that had built up on the track. Both front wheels (of the front-wheel-drive vehicle) were off the ground.

The Rescue Team managed to 'save' the Mini by all gathering around it and lifting it (with Lindi and I still inside) off the mound of dirt – amid much guffawing and snide-remarking. It was an ignoble beginning to the day which would not be forgotten and would be mentioned often for years to come.

The Rescue Team and Lindi went off to their designated areas and I waited for the next Flood Boat to transport me up the river to the site of the staged disaster.

The Flood Boat team dropped me on the bank of the river and pointed me in the direction of the first 'casualty'.

I walked up the hill and stopped to look at the simulated wounds of the casualty. To my surprise, there lay my friend from school who had been in my vivid dream. His fake wound was a broken femur (bone at the top of the leg). It was broken to the extent that the bone was protruding through a wound in the leg and fake blood was everywhere. This was a very serious injury. If the injury had been real, he would not be walking for a long while!

We were surprised to see each other and had a quick chat before I moved off to the next fake casualty. To say that "I was rattled" is an understatement. It has been thirty three years since that meeting. I haven't seen him since.

STORY TWO

This was a real party.

We had friends over for dinner. After the meal, we played cards and then some people had left and others had moved away from the table to carry on conversations. Lindi and one of the other ladies were at the table having a conversation.

I was very, very tired. I had worked a lot of overtime at work and I was also doing a course at night. I had reached the stage of near exhaustion and I was pleased that everyone was involved in conversation and no-one was missing my company.

I pretended to be listening in to the conversation next to me while I played with the cards. I broke them up into three face-down stacks. You've probably played this. The aim is just to guess which stack has the highest card at the bottom (ie facing the table).

After I had played for a while, I noticed that there was a tingling sensation in the palm of my hand when I reached for the pile of cards.

I hovered the palm of my hand over one of the piles of cards and my palm tingled again.

In my very tired state, I still found that interesting and moved my hand over the next pile of cards. My hand tingled to a different extent. I moved onto the next pile and, again, my hand tingled differently to the sensation while hovering over the other two piles.

I turned over the pile of cards that caused my hand to tingle most. Then I turned over the other two piles. The pile that had caused my hand to tingle the most was the winning (highest) card.

I played again. This time there was a significant difference in the sensation in my hand from all three piles. By the strength of the sensation, I was able to correctly choose the highest card, the next highest and the lowest.

I was really tired. This was interesting and fun but I couldn't get excited about it and I certainly wasn't going to start a conversation to tell anyone what was happening. I didn't feel like talking.

I sat there and played game after game, correctly choosing the highest card every time and often choosing the three piles in their correct sequence.

Lindi finally asked me what I was doing. I explained. I demonstrated the process to her and our friend. I continued to choose the highest card time after time. They got excited and talked excitedly about what I was doing. I woke up a bit, with the excited conversation, and from then on was unable to choose the highest card. The tingling in the palm of my hand went away. We changed the topic of conversation to other things.

This became a family game. I taught our children how to hover their palm over the piles of cards and to feel for the sensation. We all have good results but nothing like the perfect run I had on the night of our dinner party.

(If you sit at a table with either of my children and produce a pack of cards, you will probably observe them absent-mindedly hovering their hand over the pack.)

STORY THREE

My parents had a boy and a girl and were content with their family ...until I came along nine years later.

Because my brother and sister are older than me, I grew up in my teens with nephews and nieces on my hip. We have always had good relationships.

Another Dream. I didn't like this dream much. It was horrible. I dreamt that my nephew, Mark, had been involved in an accident. I woke up perspiring with a horrible feeling of death all around me. It was a vivid dream that felt predictive like the one with the school friend who was in a wheel chair.

The next day I had a phone call from my parents to say that Mark had been knocked off his skate board. It was a hit and run and he had been taken by ambulance to the hospital. I was in a sweat. Then they said "but he's OK. He's going to be alright".

I didn't believe that he was going to be alright. I was still in a panic. The feeling of 'death' in my dream was too intense for him to be alright.

Regardless of the dire warning in my dream, Mark was fine and was brought home from hospital. I was really surprised. The feeling of death was so intense in the dream. I was really relieved.

The next day Lindi and I had been out and were heading home. Our route home took us past the end of Lindi's Grandparents' street. Lindi's Aunt lived there as well. Lindi looked down the street and said jokingly "Everyone is at Nana and Pa's place. The buggers, they didn't invite us".

We hadn't been home long when the phone rang. It was Lindi's father to tell us that Lindi's Aunt had died of a Cerebral Hemorrhage that morning.

So, what is the point of the stories?

Am I trying to convince you that I am Psychic? No, actually. There have been very few moments in my life where I have had a 'knowing'. These three stories are the main events. I find myself more 'in touch' when I am regularly meditating but I don't consider myself to be psychic.

I have raised these stories for nothing more than to explain the effects that they had on me. You see, these were three events in my twenties when I 'knew' something that was beyond the normal layer of consciousness. I was told something that, by conventional thought, I should not have known. ...No-one should have known.

The obvious questions are: Who / What told me? Why was I told? How was I communicated with? Where did this knowledge of the future (in the two dreams) come from? ...And what does that infer about our choices in our lives versus pre-destiny?

I cannot answer these questions.

What I can do is tell you the effect that it had on me.

Having had these experiences, how could I now believe that there is nothing beyond this world other than what we see?

How could I not believe in Spirituality?

How could I receive these messages and not believe that there is a plan for me ...that I have a purpose? And ...if I have a purpose, why not everyone else?

I now live 'with spirit'.

Again, this is a double-edged statement. I live a spirited life, in that I am excited that my life is just an adventure. I am enjoying the adventure. I'm in the fun park! When I die, I will leave the park and go home. At home will be all the people I love who 'died' before me. How could I not now believe that?

I also live with spirit now – meaning that I know that I am a spirit having a human experience. I don't have to wait until I die to be a spirit and to feel the 'other place' where spirits belong. I am there now! I live in two dimensions. My mind is connected to that place and to those spirits.

The above will scare some people. It does have to be said, though, because it will also liberate some people.

My father died in 1983 and yet I have driven to work of a morning with the mist rising from the grass and creeks on each side of the road and the sun bathing light on a beautiful green landscape and I have felt my father's hand on my shoulder.

People who are firmly anchored in their human experience will tell me to stop talking nonsense …that I was just imagining it.

I cannot be deflected. I have had proof of spiritual experiences. I *know* there is spirit.

And I believe that I can answer at least one of the questions that I posed earlier. "Why was I told?" There was no obvious point in me knowing the information that I was given in my dreams or in knowing which card was the highest. It was trivial information that I could do nothing with. I couldn't change the events that I had been told about. The information was of no value.

The obvious reason is that I now know that someone is there to tell. It wasn't about the information. It was about the informant. There is a spirit that talked directly to my mind. As a result, I believe. As a result, when I communicate with someone during my meditation and my negative inner voice says "It is only your imagination. There's really no-one there", I can reply "Go away. ...*I know!*"

I stand on the solid rock of earth,
My mind fills the void of the Universe.

Live with Spirit.

APPENDIX A – SAMPLE AFFIRMATIONS

An Affirmation is a statement of what you want, expressed as if it already exists. Everyone should have a small list of Affirmations devoted to the areas that they want to work on – and they should be recited daily (more than once and out loud) so that the mind has an alternate opinion to the negative inner voice.

Just a warning – initially the mind will reply with something like "that's garbage" but, with persistence and repetition you will eventually make changes.

1   **I enjoy doing my affirmations each day, because they are the path to my success.**

2   **My self-talk is always positive and encouraging.**

3   **My 'talk' to my family, friends and associates is always positive and encouraging. My sphere of influence is in peace and harmony.**

4   **I love my work and, as a result, I am always positive and happy.**

5   **I am a friendly person who becomes assertive when the need arises - while retaining my own inner peace.**

6   Life is abundance. I have an abundance consciousness. (All is well in all areas of my life and in the lives of those I love).

7   I am a very healthy person. My family and I enjoy abundance in health.

8   I meditate at least once a day. This is the key to unlock a blissful existence for myself and for those I love.

9   I am resilient. All challenges are temporary and are quickly overcome - nothing stops me from achieving my goals.

10   I have a positive expectation of a successful role wherever I work. Friendship and praise result from my enthusiasm and effort.

11   I have a positive expectation of success.

12   Everything I do and say leads to the improved self-image of my family members and the people around me.

13   I have a positive, happy mind. I have a permanent smile.

14   I am cool. I am calm. I am confident.

15   I create an excellent balance between family, work, other interests and relaxation so that my life is complete and satisfying.

16   I am a very successful person with affluence in money and affluence in all other areas of life. My family's lifestyle is admired by those around us.

17   I have quality time with my beautiful family. They are the lights of my life - my encouragement for growing.

18   I retain regular contact with my close friends. (Their friendship is very important to me.)

19   I occasionally <u>plan</u> to spend time on relaxation. This is necessary alpha time. Great things will result.

20   Wherever I am, I am there 100%.

APPENDIX B – RECOMMENDED READING

Book Title	Author
Cashflow Quadrant	Robert T. Kiyosaki
Feel The Fear And Do It Anyway	Susan Jeffers
His Needs Her Needs	Willard F. Harley, Jr.
How to Win Friends & Influence People	Dale Carnegie
Men Are From Mars, Women Are From Venus	John Gray Ph.D.
Personality Plus	Florence Littauer
Real Magic	Dr Wayne Dyer
Rich Dad, Poor Dad	Robert T. Kiyosaki
The 7 Habits of Highly Effective People	Stephen R. Covey
The Five Love Languages	Gary Chapman
The Richest Man in Babylon	George S. Clason
Think and Grow Rich	Napoleon Hill
You'll See It When You Believe It	Dr Wayne Dyer

www.ingramcontent.com/pod-product-compliance
Lightning Source LLC
Chambersburg PA
CBHW060403050426
42449CB00009B/1887